Greatest
MOMENTS OF
GOLF

This edition first published in the UK in 2008
By Green Umbrella Publishing

© Green Umbrella Publishing 2008

www.gupublishing.co.uk

Publishers: Jules Gammond and Vanessa Gardner

Printed and bound in China

ISBN: 978-1-906229-77-1

The views in this book are those of the author but they are general views only and readers are urged to consult the relevant and qualified specialist
for individual advice in particular situations.

Green Umbrella Publishing hereby exclude all liability to the extent permitted by law of any errors or omissions in this book and for any loss,
damage or expense (whether direct or indirect) suffered by a third party relying on any information contained in this book.

All our best endeavours have been made to secure copyright clearance for every photograph used but in the event of any copyright owner being overlooked
please address correspondence to Green Umbrella Publishing, The Old Bakehouse, 21 The Street, Lydiard Millicent, Swindon SN5 3LU

Greatest
MOMENTS OF
GOLF

by CLAIRE WELCH

CONTENTS

CONTENTS

BOBBY JONES WINS THE GRAND SLAM IN THE SAME YEAR 1930

When Bobby Jones won the Amateur British Open on the Old Course at St Andrews in 1930 there was no such thing as the Grand Slam. But during the golfing season of 1930 Jones achieved the unthinkable and won the British Open, British Amateur, the US Open and then, on 27 September, the US Amateur. This remarkable feat was astounding to all concerned and his friend, the sports writer, OB Keeler – taking the term from the game of Bridge – coined it a Grand Slam.

So how did this remarkable sporting hero do it? Unbeknown to anyone but himself, Jones maintained his fitness throughout the previous winter and rather than hanging up his clubs – which he would have done normally – he kept golfing and played "Doug", a game invented by another of his friends, Douglas Fairbanks, which was a mixture of paddle tennis and badminton. With seemingly no more mountains to climb – Jones had already won nine major championships – he set out to win the four major championships of 1930. No other golfing great to this day has managed to obtain all four titles in just one short season.

It all started in May 1930 on the Old Course at St Andrews when Jones competed in the British Amateur championship. Faced with Cyril Tolley, the defending British Amateur champion – who was born on 17 March 1902 – in the fourth round and up against 1923 winner Roger Wethered in the final round, Jones put in a magnificent performance going six up at the 10th hole of the second 18. He remained in front through the 13th going on to win the tournament at the club he had become a member of four years previously. Interestingly, Jones was made an honorary member of the Royal & Ancient Golf Club in 1956, but insisted on continuing to pay his membership.

Then came the 65th British Open in June 1930 at the Royal Liverpool Golf Club, Hoylake. After a shaky start in the qualifying round, Jones revived his game before struggling in the third round. He finished six strokes behind Archie Compston but managed to find his form during the final round where he went on to win with a score of 75. He beat Macdonald Smith and Leo Diegel by two strokes to claim his third British Open.

BOBBY JONES WINS THE GRAND SLAM IN THE SAME YEAR

GREATEST MOMENTS OF GOLF

Jones came up against Smith three weeks later when both were competing in the US Open at Interlachen Country Club in Minneapolis. Jones struggled through the final round, but shot back with 71-73-68-75 with an overall score of 287 to pip Smith to the post by two strokes once again. The grand finale came with the US Amateur championship at Merion Cricket Club in Ardmore, Pennsylvania. The first round against Canadian Amateur champion Sandy Sommerville was to prove his toughest. But Jones was determined and with a cool head took the championship over Eugene Homans in the final round.

With four major wins in one season, Jones – who was already a hero to the golfing world – became an icon. He will be forever remembered as one of the sporting greats and for many is the world's greatest golfer ever. Jones had developed a love of golf at an early age and showed promise and natural ability. During his formative years he was also a keen baseball player and had another great friend in Babe Ruth. He was encouraged by his father to play competitive golf and at the age of six won his first tournament against other children by displaying a maturity way beyond his years. Aged nine he defeated a 16-year-old opponent to win the Atlanta Athletic Club junior title and four years later won the invitational tournament at Birmingham, Alabama.

More wins saw Jones become the youngest ever player to compete in the 1916 Amateur championship at the Merion Cricket Club in Ardmore – perhaps fitting then that it would be here some 14 years later that he would claim the first ever Grand Slam. As an astonishing player Jones faced increasing public expectations but this was nothing compared to the pressure that the young golfer put himself under and the perfectionist in him struggled with his early volatile temper.

In 1921 Jones visited the UK and the Old Course at St Andrews for the first time with fellow Americans to play British counterparts in a tournament that was to become the Walker Cup a year later. After particularly bad play on the Old Course, Jones withdrew from the tournament and received some harsh press exposure. The experience was to mark a turning point for the golfer. Experience and composure came with age and slowly but surely Jones found his exceptional form winning his first major tournament in 1923 at the US Open at Inwood Country Club, New York. It was to prove the start of an exceptional career that would see the earlier disillusioned young player become one of the greatest sporting legends the world has ever seen. He died on 18 December 1971 and the world lost a hero.

BEN HOGAN WINS THE MASTERS, US OPEN AND THE OPEN 1953

Although it did not happen in the same year, Ben Hogan became the second player ever to achieve a Grand Slam. The year was 1953 and Hogan was the hot favourite to win the British Open at Carnoustie. The Golf Club hadn't hosted the Open for 16 years and record crowds of 27,000 turned out to see the Irish-American champion play.

That he did play was somewhat of a miracle as Hogan had suffered serious injuries in a car crash in 1949 that saw him travel little. But spurred on by his victories in the Masters and the US Open that same season, Hogan was determined to compete. The championship saw him win with a score of 282.

Hogan's Grand Slam was not completed in the same season as the PGA Championship of 1953 was played from 1-7 July while Carnoustie was hosting the British Open from 6-10 July. With a one-day overlap Hogan couldn't play both tournaments and, encouraged by his fellow professionals, he chose the Open. Of the six tournaments that Hogan entered in 1953 he won five – three of them major championships. Arriving just two weeks before the Open, Hogan set out to prepare for his game. He was unaccustomed to the British golf ball which was smaller than the US golf ball at 1.62 inches. He was surprised to find that the smaller ball gave him a much longer strike – more than 15 yards longer – than its US counterpart and Hogan, renowned for practice, was devilish in his pursuit of perfection. Using a two iron Hogan won the championship. Despite winning he did not return to defend his title the following year and in fact the tournament at Carnoustie was to be his last Open championship.

Hogan had suffered horrific injuries during the car crash of 1949 which left some doubt as to whether the champion golfer would ever walk again never mind kick-start his illustrious career. But undeterred by his fractured pelvis, fractured collar bone and left ankle, chipped rib and terrifying blood clots, Hogan fought back and regained some strength that saw him back on the golf course in 1950 where, although a frail former shadow of himself, his incredible play saw him force a play-off with "Slamming" Sammy Snead which he won. This was to be the start of a career that saw

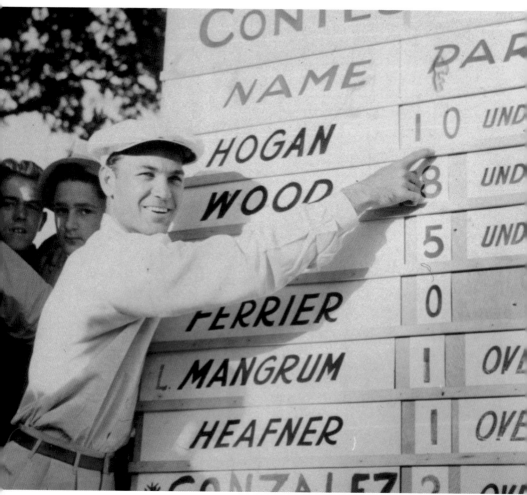

BEN HOGAN WINS THE MASTERS, US OPEN AND THE OPEN

Hogan shine and his years between 1950 and 1953 are hailed by most as his best. The crash had left Hogan with some painful injuries that saw him carefully choose the tournaments he entered and as the best US champion on the golf course he was criticised for not attending more matches. He was a steely, determined man who disliked pomp and circumstance and was a private man who would not be ruled by the politics of the day. So where did it all begin?

Hogan was brought up by his mother with his two siblings following the suicide of his father. Born in Dublin, Texas on 13 August 1912 he worked at odd jobs to bring some income into the family home. He was a caddy and later a bank clerk before his destiny took hold and he became a professional golfer during the 1930s. He had moderate success although he also had a great many losses during this time and his career did not resemble that of legends. Today, with the money available to golfing champions, practising the game of golf is a pre-requisite, but during the 1930s and 1940s it was pretty much unheard of. However, Hogan was renowned for the lonely time he spent practising his game and this is what probably turned him into one of golf's sporting legends. Perhaps marred by a more difficult than most childhood, Hogan learnt to focus, to concentrate and to put in the effort needed to get results. His steely reserve earned him the nickname the "Ice Man" from the Scottish crowds at Carnoustie who were genuinely wowed by his performance but Hogan had a positive outlook on life – despite the Hogan glare which earned him his other nickname "The Hawk" – and quickly established himself with wins, including the US Open, the PGA Championship and numerous US inter-state Open tournaments throughout the 1940s.

Fiercely competitive, Hogan had developed his legendary swing over many years. He was to become the greatest ball striker to have ever played golf having practised for many hours to perfect the swing that left his opponents wilting. It was designed to perform under pressure, and with his non-verbal competition tactic and his seemingly nerveless demeanour, the swing made Hogan a formidable opponent. He gained many critics throughout his career, but mostly for the off-hand comments he made rather than for his game, and he remains to this day one of the most influential golfers to have graced the courses of the US. Hogan died on 25 July 1997 but will be forever remembered as the "perfectionist" of golf.

GARY PLAYER, THIRD MAN TO WIN ALL FOUR MAJORS
1965

Born on 1 November 1935 in Johannesburg, South Africa, Gary Player became only the third man ever to win the four major championships and be eligible for the title of Grand Slam winner. He was brought up by his father from the age of eight – his mother Muriel died from cancer – and had a set of clubs which were paid for by a loan his father took out to enable the young Player to begin his stunning career. Player is crowned with having the most professional wins and is one of the most successful golfers of all time.

So how did this young boy from Johannesburg become one of golf's brightest stars?

At the age of 14 Player faced his first real opponent in a round of golf that saw him par the first three holes. Three years later he became a professional golfer, a route that was to see him compared with the likes of Palmer and Nicklaus to become one of the "Big Three" – a sporting hero whose success was high profile during the late 1950s through to the early 1970s. Player headed for the US during the late 1950s where he was a regular on the PGA tour including winning the 1958 Kentucky Derby Open. He won the British Open in 1959 but the following year was back in the US where he claimed victories in the Lucky International, the Sunshine Open and the Masters. The following year saw him claim the PGA Championship title among others.

Like Palmer, Player's career began at the start of televised golf and this quickly established him as a household name, nicknamed "The Black Knight" for the black attire he wore on the courses. His early touring days were spent in the company of his wife Vivienne and his six children who travelled with Player across the world and back on a regular basis – in fact, to date, Player is accredited with travelling more than 14 million miles during his prolific career.

Having gained victories in the Masters, PGA Championship and the British Open, all Player needed was the US Open to gain the famous Grand Slam. In 1964 he found himself in fifth place behind Palmer at the Masters and in eighth position at the British Open behind winner Tony Lema. But the following year, 1965, was to see Player take the Grand Slam when he won the US Open at Bellerive Cricket Club in St Louis, Missouri. After four rounds the South African hero was

GARY PLAYER, THIRD MAN TO WIN ALL FOUR MAJORS

level with Australian competitor Kel Nagle with scores of 70, 70, 71 and 71. Player triumphed in the play-off with Nagle when he beat his opponent by three strokes with a score of 71. Not only did Player achieve the Grand Slam, he was also the first non-US player to win the US Open since Ted Ray from the UK claimed victory in 1920. It had taken Player six years to achieve his Grand Slam – which was bettered by Jack Nicklaus who subsequently managed it in four years, and of course, the legendary Bobby Jones who achieved it in five short months in 1930 and was the start of it all.

Despite his Grand Slam and the success of the US Open in 1965, Player did not win another major tournament until he lifted the trophy at the British Open in Carnoustie in 1968. But it didn't seem to matter to the fans of Player who watched eagerly as he came fourth at the Open in 1966 (just four strokes behind Jack Nicklaus) and achieved third place in the PGA Championship that same year. He also gained third place at the Open at Hoylake the following year when a disappointing final round saw eventual winner Roberto de Vicenzo take the title with a seven-stroke lead over Player. Player was also the only competitor during the 20th century to win the British Open in three different decades.

However, hailing from South Africa the Ryder Cup was never open to Player, although he was eligible to take part in the international team playing for the President's Cup in 2003 – a similar event – which was hosted by the Links in George, South Africa on a course that Player himself designed. The 2005 President's Cup saw Player's team lose to the US by three points but the golfing great competed against Jack Nicklaus's team at the 2007 match in September at the Royal Montreal Golf Club in Canada which saw the Americans win by 19 1/2 to 14 1/2. Gary Player's success was not just confined to his own abilities as a professional golfer and he is renowned as a golf course architect and has designed more than 200 courses worldwide. He also founded Black Knight International (incorporating Gary Player Equipment, Gary Player Academy and Gary Player Enterprises) as well as the Gary Player Stud Farm and the Player Foundation which promotes education.

JACK NICKLAUS DEFENDS MASTERS AND WINS GRAND SLAM 1966

It had taken the legendary Jack Nicklaus just four years to claim his Grand Slam victory when he defended his Masters championship title and then won the Open at Muirfield in a dazzling display of talent in 1966. At the time, the Open was the only major tournament to have eluded the golfing giant, but the "Golden Bear" as he was nicknamed staved off the challenge from Doug Sanders and Dave Thomas to claim the championship in a convincing win. Nicklaus was so pleased with the achievement that he went on to name his own course Muirfield Village in Dublin, Ohio.

It was to be the first of three victories for Nicklaus at the Open. When Thomas and Sanders both took a par at the 17th hole, Nicklaus needed two fours to win. Having been runner-up at the tournament a total of seven times, Nicklaus was determined and on form to win. At the 17th, knowing that not much lay between him and the championship, Nicklaus scored a birdie four and par four on the final two holes to finish one stroke ahead of his rivals.

Nicklaus, born on 21 January 1940, began his road to the Grand Slam when he won the US Open in 1962 beating Arnold Palmer in a play-off. The following year saw him win the Masters with a one-stroke lead over Tony Lema while later in 1963 he claimed his first PGA Championship title when he triumphed over Dave Ragan Jr with a two-stroke lead. All he needed was the British Open. But 1965 did not prove to be his defining year although he did win the Masters for the second time with a nine-stroke lead over challengers Arnold Palmer and Gary Player. The Masters was once again a victory for Nicklaus in 1966 after he found himself up against Gay Brewer and Tommy Jacobs in a play-off that was to see the "Golden Bear" win. However later that same year he proved just how much of a sporting hero he was when he claimed his Grand Slam.

JACK NICKLAUS DEFENDS MASTERS AND WINS GRAND SLAM 19

JACK NICKLAUS DEFENDS MASTERS AND WINS GRAND SLAM

Hailing from Columbus, Ohio, Nicklaus took up golf at the age of 10 and by the age of 13 was competent enough on the course to score 70. Three years later saw him claim his first Ohio State Open against professionals in 1956 and within another five years – while still at Ohio State University – he won victories in two US Amateur Championships (1959 and 1961). The 1960 US Open saw Nicklaus as runner-up to Arnold Palmer – only two shots behind and 1959 and 1961 were also the years that Nicklaus represented the US in the Walker Cup team where he won all his matches. At the time Nicklaus won the US Open in 1962 – his first year as a professional – beating Arnold Palmer, he was the youngest winner in the history of the tournament. The year was to prove a flying start for the exceptional golfer who went on to win the Seattle Open and the Portland Open that same year. His efforts earned him the "Rookie of the Year" award. Other major tournaments were victories for Nicklaus the following year and although he did not win any majors during 1964 he did find himself at the top of the tour money list over Arnold Palmer.

Things really took off for him when he won the Masters in 1965 and then again in 1966. It was the first time that any golfer had managed to successfully defend the title. Nicklaus was on the up and by the time he won the Grand Slam in 1966 he was only the fourth professional to achieve it after Ben Hogan, Gene Sarazen and Gary Player.

Things quietened down for Nicklaus on the world's golf courses after 1967 and he failed to win another major until the British Open in 1970 on the Old Course at St Andrews where he beat rival Doug Sanders in a play-off. (He became a member of the Royal & Ancient Club 20 years later). The following year was to see him win the 1971 PGA Championship which gave Nicklaus the honour of being the first golfer to win all four major championships twice. During the remainder of the 1970s and the 1980s Nicklaus continued with an incredible game of golf that contemporaries marvelled at. He joined the Champions Tour at the age of 50 in 1990 and enjoyed success until 1992 which proved to be a winless year for the "Golden Bear". He was back on form the following year and enjoyed a busy decade on the greens.

He came back to compete in the 2005 Masters and finished his sensational career at the Open on the Old Course at St Andrews that same year although he did take part in the US Open and the PGA Championship in 2000. This great sporting hero is also a talented and devoted architect of golf courses and currently has one of the largest golf design companies in the world.

TONY JACKLIN WINS THE BRITISH OPEN 1969

Quite simply, Tony Jacklin was the hero of British golf from 1969 to 1972. He popularised the sport for the masses in the UK with his epic win of the Open in 1969 then again when he went on to triumph at the US Open in 1970. This made him the first player to hold both British and US titles simultaneously since 1953 when Ben Hogan was champion of both.

With a focused game, hundreds of hours of lone practice and the imagination to think that Ben Hogan was watching every move he made, Jacklin's hard work reaped the rewards when he stepped onto the course at Royal Lytham. No British player had won the Open since Max Faulkner in 1951 – but Jacklin was about to change all that. Born in Scunthorpe on 7 July 1944, Jacklin was a keen golfer from an early age. Jacklin's father was a lorry driver but in his spare time had a love of golf that he passed to his young son. His style developed well and he was decisive and expertly controlled his game from 100 yards inwards. He possessed an aggressive style of attack which made him formidable against opponents but his parents were worried about him becoming a professional – with the risks it involved – despite his resounding successes at the Lincolnshire Championships. However, aged 17, Jacklin was offered an assistant professional job at Potters Bar by Bill Shankland and the young lad from Scunthorpe couldn't arrive fast enough. Although he worked hard for Shankland, the long tedious hours didn't really enthral or inspire the young professional and he was keen for more exciting endeavours.

He was to get his wish. At Royal Lytham, spectators were anxious for an exciting result. Jacklin scored impressively in the first and second rounds with 68 and 70 respectively and by the third round he was only three strokes behind Bob Charles – the Open Champion of 1963. By the final round Jacklin had increased his form enough to be two strokes ahead of

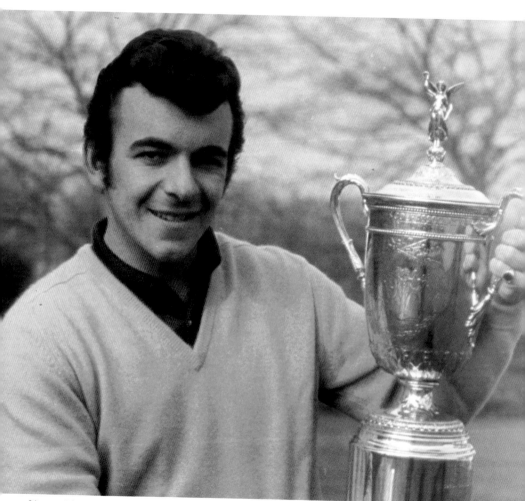

TONY JACKLIN WINS THE BRITISH OPEN

Charles. Bob Charles watched as his ball went into the rough on the final hole, while Jacklin sent his drive down the middle of the fairway. Charles was back on the green by his second shot but Jacklin's second shot took him closer to the green. It took Jacklin just two putts to triumph over rival Charles and take the 1969 Championship. As a result of his achievement – he was the first British golfer to win the tournament in 18 years – Jacklin's popularity soared and the British public took up golf, watched golf, practised golf and breathed golf in their droves. He was the Arnold Palmer – one of his own heroes – of the British game. Jacklin was in with a chance of winning the Open once again in 1972 when he and Lee Trevino tied for the lead one stroke ahead of Jack Nicklaus at the 17th hole. Jacklin was in just as much disbelief as everyone else – including Trevino – when Trevino's ball (which had hit the upslope behind the green) was hit by a frustrated challenger who watched as the ball rolled straight into the hole for a par.

Not only did Jacklin hit the heights with his brilliant win at the Open in 1969 but he also impressed the world of golf with his outstanding performance in the Ryder Cup of that same year. This was also one of the most memorable performances in the Ryder Cup's history and is known to golf fans the world over as "The Concession". It was down to Jacklin and his fellow competitor in the final singles match of the tournament to decide which side of the Atlantic would be celebrating a win. Not fazed by the magnitude of the moment, Jacklin kept his cool to deliver a 50-foot eagle putt at the 17th at Royal Birkdale which put the British and Irish team in good contention for the title. It led to a tie – the first for the Ryder Cup – although Nicklaus retained the Cup for the US. It was a moving and memorable moment when two golfing giants walked off the 18th green with their arms around each other's shoulders. This is probably one of the greatest shows of professionalism ever and is widely regarded by all who witnessed it as a grand gesture of true sportsmanship.

Jacklin became the Ryder Cup captain for the British and Irish team in 1983. This role was to transform the tournament into what it has become today and no other player in the history of the Cup has done more than Jacklin to see it transcend to the heady heights it occupies in the golfing calendar. Indeed, for Jacklin, "The Ryder Cup is more than just golf. It is your country, your team, your tour, your captain, you're playing for it…it is the ultimate in golf". When Jacklin took over the captaincy in 1983, the US team had been, and still was, threatening to dominate the tournament. Although the British and Irish lost that year it somehow ignited a fire – fanned by Jacklin – for the team to succeed in the future. Two years later Jacklin was an inspiration for his team as non-playing captain and the British team won the Ryder Cup for the first time in 28 years.

JACK NICKLAUS'S "DUEL IN THE SUN" WITH TOM WATSON 1977

Golf is often at its most exciting when renowned competitors are left behind and the competition turns into a head to head between two leading stars who are battling it out all the way to the 18th. Often referred to as "duels", one such compelling match involved Jack Nicklaus in a show-down with Tom Watson. The year was 1977 and the setting was the course at Turnberry when the two men found themselves locked in a battle for the Open Championship – it was quickly dubbed the "Duel in the Sun". They had challenged each other over two days before fighting their way down the back nine on the final day. It is still considered today as possibly the greatest head-to-head of all time.

Tom Watson's second stroke at the 14th gave him a perfect drop to the green while Jack Nicklaus's (born 21 January 1940) shot down the fairway rivalled that of his opponent. Nicklaus's follow-up shot turned just shy of the hole and Watson had a chance to draw level. It wasn't to be as both players misjudged the slight slope leading to the hole from their respective sides on the green. By the time Nicklaus made the hole on the next shot he was 10 under par and one stroke ahead of Watson. From the tee at the 15th Nicklaus made the green, narrowly missing the new bunker, while the American Watson's (born 4 September 1949) putt from the edge of the green rolled the ball easily into the hole. With three holes left to play the "duel" was heating up as the players became level.

The crowd was stunned at the 16th when Nicklaus's seemingly final putt – which he hit straight at the left side – narrowly missed its destination. His next putt was easily in the hole, but Watson's following shot took him into the lead for the first time in the match. He maintained his form when his second stroke onto the green at the 18th landed perfectly positioned for a simple putt to win – all eyes were now on the golfer from Kansas City, Missouri to take the championship.

JACK NICKLAUS'S "DUEL IN THE SUN" WITH TOM WATSON

Watson needed to miss and Nicklaus needed to put the ball in the hole if there was to be a tie in front of the 23,000 spectators positioned around the green at the 18th. Nicklaus achieved an incredible putt to put the ball in the hole, but it wasn't to be enough and Tom Watson's final putt gave him the "Duel in the Sun" victory.

The 1970s and 1980s were to be Tom Watson's most memorable golfing decades and he was ranked the world's number one golfer by McCormack from 1978 to 1982. The following two years saw him trail behind Seve Ballesteros but only just. He began his career in 1971 and went on to win eight major tournaments including two Masters (in 1977 and 1981), the US Open in 1987 and five British Open championships in 1975, 1977 ("Duel in the Sun"), 1980, 1982 and 1983. Watson won't just be remembered for his triumphant win over Nicklaus at Turnberry in Scotland.

His US Open victory five years later at Pebble Beach was also to become a talking point when he once again found himself tied with Nicklaus at the 17th hole. Watson's tee shot went into the rough but his chip shot incredibly hit the flagstick and holed the shot – giving him a birdie – where he went on to win by two strokes. The 2003 US Open was another highlight in Watson's already prolific career when he opened the first round with a promising score of 65.

His game was somewhat revived – after a period of decline – during the 1990s. He became part of the Champions Tour at the end of the 1990s and became an honorary member of the Royal & Ancient Club at St Andrews – although he never claimed an Open victory on the Old Course. He also has been honoured with being named as the PGA Player of the Year six times and in 1987 was awarded the Bobby Jones Award which is the highest award given by the USGA in recognition of his sportsmanship in the game of golf. He was entered into the World Golf Hall of Fame in 1988.

Watson has won 39 PGA Tour awards which began with a confident victory at the Western Open in 1974. He followed it with the Byron Nelson Golf Classic and the Open Championship in 1975 before winning his first Masters tournament – among many other tournaments – in 1977 along with his historic win at Turnberry. As well as the major tournaments, Watson is also no stranger to the golf courses of the world having won the 1980 Dunlop Phoenix championship in Japan, the 1984 Australian Open, the Hong Kong Open in 1992 and the Dunlop Phoenix once again in 1997. He holds several Champions Tour titles – nine in total – including the 2000 IR Senior Tour Championship, the 2001 Senior PGA Championship, the 2003 Senior Open Championship and 2005 Senior Open Championship to name but a few.

GARY PLAYER, BEST EVER SCORE TO WIN THE MASTERS
1978

South African Gary Player has won 160 professional tournaments in his illustrious career and has travelled more than 14 million miles around the world. His achievements include 24 PGA Tour wins which span 20 years and more than 100 other non-senior golfing tournaments. He won the Australian Open seven times between 1958 and 1974 and has a total of 18 wins on the Australasian Tour between 1956 and 1981. Between 1955 and 1981 he clocked up 73 wins on the South African Tour (now called the Sunshine Tour) including victories at 13 South African Opens. He has won many Champions Tour trophies including three Senior PGA Tour Championships (1986, 1988 and 1990) along with the US Senior Open which he won on two occasions in 1987 and 1988. He also went on to win the Senior British Open three times in 1988, 1990 and 1997. However, his historic victory at the Masters in 1978 will be forever etched on the memory of the golfing world.

It would be the third Masters victory for Player and many were doubtful of his ability to achieve success at Augusta National Golf Club as he had been described as past his prime. He was really up against the competition in the final round but Player astounded the crowds when he orchestrated a miracle when his second shot at the 15th hole landed across the water and safely on the green with an eagle putt. He birdied the 9th, 10th and 13th holes to achieve a score of eight under par at the 15th. His excellent 80-foot putt took him within a comfortable distance of the hole. However it was a tricky putt that he safely delivered into the hole on the 15th to secure a joint first place position. It took him to the 16th hole with a score of nine under par. By the 17th hole he was 10 under par and needed an excellent putt to take him into the lead. It was the first time in the four-day tournament that he had a shot at victory and Player wasn't about to lose his focus. His putt on the 18th gave him a score of 64 for the round – it was a "course record" – one that still hasn't been equalled to this day. On the course to congratulate him was Seve Ballesteros. The birdie at the 18th hole and 11 under par had done it for Player with a final score of 64, 71, 78. The runners-up included Hubert Green, Watson and Funseth all at 10 under par.

GARY PLAYER, BEST EVER SCORE TO WIN THE MASTERS

The Masters Tournament, fondly known as the Masters, is the first in the season each year and unlike other major men's championships is only ever held in one place – Augusta National Golf Club. Designed by Bobby Jones and the great architect Alister MacKenzie, the course champions are automatically invited to play at the US Open, the Open and the PGA Championship for the following five years. Champions at Augusta are also invited to play at the Masters for life – although the field at this tournament is slightly smaller than most other majors with only around 90 players or so.

The tournament is held over four days and 72 holes and although the event follows the rules as set out by the United States Golf Association there are also special rulings at Augusta that are defined by the Masters Tournament Committee. As the field is relatively small for a golfing tournament it is traditional at the Masters for groups of three players to play the first 36 holes – usually over the Thursday and Friday – while a cut is then made once all players have participated in the first 36 holes. Another regulation of the Committee was that all players had to use the services of an Augusta National Club caddy although this was relaxed in 1983 and since then professionals have been eligible to use their own caddies.

The Masters originally began as the "Augusta National Invitational Tournament" at the insistence of a humble Bobby Jones, but in 1939 the legendary golfer relented and the tournament became known as the Masters Tournament. The first Masters played the current holes from numbers 10 to 18 as the first nine while numbers one to nine were traditionally the second nine. Despite the common usage of the front and back nine, Augusta has tended to stick with the original choice of first and second nine when referring to the holes.

Controversy reigned in 2006 when the course was lengthened from 6,850 yards to 7,445 yards. The change drew fierce criticism from legendary players such as Jack Nicklaus, Arnold Palmer and Tiger Woods among others. However, three times Masters Champion Gary Player defended the changes. Player courted controversy himself with the golf club that actively discourages older players from participating in the Masters today. Player took no notice and challenged other competitors when he took part in the 2006 tournament at the age of 70.

Gary Player was the first non-US Master Champion in 1961 so it is perhaps fitting for this great sporting hero to hold the record of the lowest score on the course.

FIRST RYDER CUP FEATURING A EUROPEAN SIDE
1979

The first ever non UK or Irish players to grace the team for the Ryder Cup were Seve Ballesteros and fel Spaniard Antonio Garrido in 1979. Since the first Ryder Cup back in 1927 – initiated by merchant Sam Ryder – until the end of the 1970s, the two teams consisted of just US, British and Irish participants. To Jacklin took over as captain in 1983 (although he had played in many Ryder Cups between 1967 and 1979). It was Jacklin who inspired change and Jacklin who turned the Ryder Cup into the focused and prestigious event that it is today.

From 1979 onwards – even though many other European nations were not part of the Ryder Cup un 1985 onwards – the event had a more European flavour for the British and Irish team who found that inclusion of other nations to their team helped to even the balance as US domination was beginning to wane. In 1983 at Palm Beach, Jacklin as captain of the European side, managed to coax Ballesteros bac into the team.

The Spanish legend had famously refused to play in the tournament again after a row with the European Tour over appearance money. He had then been left out of the side in the 1981 event as it wa argued that his extended time in the States left him ineligible to play for the European team. Ballestero agreed to participate in 1983 and partnered rookie Paul Way. Ballesteros put in a memorable performa – especially with his shot from the fairway bunker on the 18th – and helped the European team to gain more success.

Despite outstanding play from the side Jacklin's team lost in 1983 by one point but in 1985 at the Belfry they began to ring the changes when the home side won for the first time since 1957 under Britis captain Dai Rees. Jacklin demanded first class treatment for the team which made him popular among players and helped to enhance the professionalism of the event.

Ballesteros' involvement in the tournament was almost as legendary as Jacklins' from the early to mid 1980s onwards. He famously partnered Jose Maria Olazabal in 1987 and then David Gilford almost 10 years later. He became captain himself in 1997 when the Ryder Cup went to Spain for the first time and the European side defended their trophy with a one-point victory.

FIRST RYDER CUP FEATURING A EUROPEAN SIDE

However the Ryder Cup hasn't been without its controversial matches and in 1969 – before European involvement – Royal Birkdale was the setting for such a match. It was a competitive tournament by any standards but there was additional acrimony and unsporting elements from some players. Jack Nicklaus angered fellow team members and captain Sammy Snead when he conceded a two-footer to Tony Jacklin after a four-footer for par on the last green. It was Nicklaus's first Ryder Cup and the US retained the title.

Then, 22 years later, Ballesteros and Paul Azinger accused each other of cheating at the Belfry in 1991. It led to a memorable pairs match with the Spaniard and his fellow countryman Olazabal winning. Eight years later saw another controversial match at the Country Club in Brookline in the US after the home team fought a remarkable comeback to win a one-point victory over the European side having trailed behind at 10-6 at the start of the final day. It was the team's first victory since 1993. Olazabal was up against Leonard and after the American made a dramatic putt at the 17th fans streamed onto the course. The Spaniard still had his putt to take and tried to regain his focus. The putt did not go well for Olazabal and once again the US contingent celebrated – although more modestly this time. It was decided that no rules had been broken – however unfortunate it had been for the European team member. The European team felt that a number of unwritten rules had been ignored although the US team denied this and stated that the reaction was hypocritical. Captain Mark James was less than amused with events and there remained some considerable bad blood between the opposing sides. Some of the US team later apologised and both sides tried to play down the event. It seems to have worked and subsequent matches have truly been "in the spirit of the game".

One such game was the 2006 match which the European team won for the third time in succession with an 18½ to 9½ victory (the same result that was achieved in the 2004 event). European captain, Ian Woosnam's team had a four-point lead going into the final day whereupon they promptly dominated the singles matches for the entire day. Darren Clarke at the 16th was particularly outstanding and went on to win his match against Zach Johnson of the US. It was a poignant and moving moment as fans rushed on to the green to congratulate the recently widowed player. Clarke's wife had died of cancer just six weeks before the event. In an extraordinary show of courage and determination Clarke had been integral in his team's winning achievements and the cheering crowds saw the sporting hero break down in tears. Woosnam's inspiration as captain is legendary and the team equalled their biggest winning score.

EUROPE CLAIM THE RYDER CUP 1985

Battling it out since 1926, the British and Irish team (who became the European Tour team in 1985 – although players from other nations were included from 1979) and the US have enjoyed peaks and troughs throughout the history of the Ryder Cup. The year of 1985 – with Seve Ballesteros having been coaxed back into the team two years previously by captain Tony Jacklin – was to see the US lose the trophy for the first time since 1957.

The US team, hoping to defend their nine victories since 1959, could have been forgiven for thinking that the result was a sure thing. But the hard work put in by the European team was about to render the US team disappointed for the first time in 28 years. In 1957 the British and Irish team pulled off an unlikely victory in the Ryder Cup when Christie O'Connor drove off the tee on the final day for the home side at Lindrick in Ireland. The team under the captaincy of Dai Rees were not given much of a chance of beating the dominant US team. Great Britain and Eire started the singles 3-1 down. However the Americans found the pace too hot at Lindrick and their opponents – who included the likes of Peter Mills playing in his first Ryder Cup match – were playing like champions. In the singles matches the US only won one of their games – all the rest went to the challengers.

In 1985, European captain Tony Jacklin insisted on preparation and professionalism from team members – something that was to stand them in good stead. The team effort was paramount and went on to produce one of the most memorable images in golfing history. The score was 13-8 to the European team, courtesy of Paul Way, as Sam Torrance took to the green elsewhere for a short putt that could produce a birdie and win the hole. Torrance was triumphant when he achieved just that on the 17th hole.

He followed it with a huge drive down the fairway in pursuit of the 18th hole and waited patiently while his opponent took his shot. Torrance only needed one more to win the trophy. Andy North's tee shot found the lake and the anxious faces of the US spectators were plain to see. Sam Torrance prepared himself to shoot the ball over the water at the 18th. A comfortable shot saw him make the green with only a few feet between the ball and victory. Torrance made history when the ball found the hole with just one putt. Jacklin, the European team and their supporters were elated. After 28 years the Europeans had finally done it. It was to pave the way for more exciting Ryder Cups to come.

Two years later saw the European team in the States where they retained their crown thanks to the likes of Seve Ballesteros and Jose Maria Olazabal. These two sporting giants along with the rest of the team were to lay the foundations for a 15-13 win. It was pinned on Larry Nelson at the 18th hole who needed to somehow win the hole in order for the US to have a realistic chance of winning the trophy back again. Nelson's decisive chip from the rough just short of the green was clean and smooth, but just not powerful enough and the ball landed a little to one side of the cup. The final putt came from Seve Ballesteros who stood up from collecting his ball from the hole looking ecstatic. The home crowd were as pleased for the visitors as the supporters that had travelled from Europe. It was a successful tournament for the European team who had started to even the balance of power with a consecutive win.

The European team were triumphant once again in 2002 when the Ryder Cup was hosted at the Belfry. Harrington took the European team three up with a birdie putt at the end of the front nine. Colin Montgomerie continued the trend when he bagged a possible four out of five points at the end of his round at the 14th hole. Team members Langer, Harrington, Bjorn and Fasth all looked good after day one and it was incumbent on the Americans to step up their pace. Phil Price made a promising start against Phil Mickelson. However he struggled at the 395 par four 6th hole while Mickelson made it all look so easy landing comfortably on the green. Price struck back and landed neatly just yards from the hole. Harrington meanwhile on the par three 14th hole needed a putt to win his match. He duly delivered and the home side were progressing well. Langer faced the same situation as Harrington when he reached the par five hole at the 15th. Like Harrington he won the match. However, it wasn't all easy on the fairways and many of the players on both teams found some moments difficult. Westwood conceded defeat to American Verplank on the 17th green while Mickelson was eventually beaten by Price. The Americans still trailed two points behind when the score reached 12½ to 10½. The match ended 15½ to 12½.

JACK NICKLAUS, THE OLDEST MASTERS WINNER AT 46 1986

At the "grand old age" of 46, Jack Nicklaus stepped onto the course at Augusta National in 1986 to become the oldest professional golfer to win the Masters tournament. His final round of 65 gave him his last major tournament before he joined the Champions Tour. However also celebrating that day was Nick Price who scored a course record of 63.

Nicklaus was the best of his time with nothing else to prove but he went on to claim the Masters in 1986 with a performance of pure genius – it was a fitting tribute to the man who had shown time and time again that he was a master of his craft. He made a putt for an eagle on the 15th green which took him level with Tom Kite and into second place at seven under par. His putt at the 17th took him nine under par and the roar from the crowd was simply deafening. At the 18th tee he faced the formidable tunnel of trees and numerous bunkers on the challenging course to make the fairway. He succeeded of course with a comfortable shot. His second shot to the green made it safely but Nicklaus was faced with the large hump in the green which he needed to overcome in order to achieve his victory. It was a misjudgement by the great golfer but his putt on the green over the hump took him incredibly only inches from the hole. His next putt gave him a score of 65 – Nick Price had already achieved his round of 63 earlier in the day – and it was a case of wait and see as Greg Norman followed behind. At the 17th Norman needed a putt for a birdie to take him nine under par to tie with Jack Nicklaus with only one hole left to play. The "Great White Shark" and the "Golden Bear" were tied as Norman polished off the hole with great finesse.

Sadly for Norman his second shot down the fairway on the 18th found its way into the spectator stands rather than the green – similar to his second shot at the 18th the previous year at the US Open – and Norman looked set for defeat. He needed to make the hole from the grandstand in two strokes to enable him to tie with Nicklaus and bring about a sudden-death play-off. The first shot was a little too high, although it did leave Norman with a chance when it landed safely on the green. His putt missed the hole and Nicklaus became the 1986 Masters Champion. Norman finished one stroke behind.

JACK NICKLAUS, THE OLDEST MASTERS WINNER AT 46

Steeped in history the Masters begins with an honorary opening tee shot by one of golf's sporting legends. Sam Snead began the Masters tournament on the historic day that Nicklaus won in 1986. Caddies who accompany the players at this prestigious event are required to wear a white jumpsuit complete with a green Masters cap and white tennis shoes while the jumpsuit sports the surname of the player they are supporting. As Bobby Jones was the co-designer (with Alister MacKenzie) of Augusta and the initiator of the Masters the tournament has a strong tradition of honouring amateur golf by inviting the champions of the elite amateur tournaments around the world to participate in the Masters itself. The Silver Cup is presented to the lowest scoring amateur in the tournament to make the cut. The cup, introduced in 1952, was joined by the Silver Medal which was introduced two years later for the lowest scoring runner-up. The runner-up of the overall tournament receives a silver medal while the winner receives a gold medal, cash award and the Green Jacket.

The jacket has been awarded to champions at Augusta since 1949 and is highly coveted by the golfing professionals lucky enough to receive one. The jacket is also the official coat worn by Augusta National members while on Club grounds and each Masters winner becomes an honorary member. Sam Snead was the first Masters Champion to receive the Green Jacket in 1949 but the rules of the club stipulate that the winner may only remove the jacket from the premises for the first year after a win. After 12 months the jacket must be returned to the club for the honorary members to wear whenever they return to the club. To date, Gary Player is the only Masters winner who failed to return his Green Jacket to the Club, despite insistence that this was against club rules.

In keeping with tradition it is usual for the previous year's winner to put the Green Jacket on the winner who succeeds them. When Jack Nicklaus won the tournament consecutively in 1995 and 1966 he put the jacket on himself in the latter year. This was changed in following tournaments to allow the chairman of the Augusta National to put the Green Jacket on successive winners such as Nick Faldo in 1990 (who won in 1989) and Tiger Woods after his second victory in 2002.

NICK FALDO WINS THE OPEN 1987

Home to the Honourable Company of Edinburgh Golfers, Muirfield is the oldest golf club in the world, founded in 1744. The course is hugely demanding and its dangers are obvious. The top golfers have long considered Muirfield to be a fair test of ability in championship golf and so perhaps it is fitting that Nick Faldo should win the Open here in 1987. Faldo managed to par all 18 holes in his final round at the tournament to secure his first Open victory.

Muirfield is a 6,801-yard par 70 course and like all the courses at Gullane is hilly with characteristic heather and gorse. There are also demanding downhill holes that require a focused mind – although these are more like those to be found on an inland course rather than a links course. Muirfield, like many other famous links (and inland courses), was designed by Old Tom Morris and the current course opened in 1891. The course has played host to the Open Championship on 15 occasions, the last time in 2002, when Ernie Els won his first Open victory.

Back to 1987 and Faldo set out to claim his first Open Championship on the final day. It wasn't to be all plain sailing though and his third shot at the 17th saw his ball roll down a hilly bank and into the edge of the rough by the green. The putt didn't have quite enough power behind it and the ball swung away from the hole on the sloping green. Faldo at this point was five under par and in second place behind Paul Azinger who was six under par at the 16th hole but the American's lead was only a slender one stroke ahead. Faldo meanwhile was struggling to get a birdie. Although he had had several chances to achieve a birdie he just hadn't managed to. The weather was more a hindrance than a help and by the time Faldo reached the 17th hole a thick mist hung over Muirfield threatening to envelop the tournament.

Faldo's drive from the 18th tee was impressive but what also helped was that Azinger's tee shot from the 17th ended up in a small but deep bunker. His only choice was to get the ball out sideways which he managed comfortably. With only 195 yards to go Faldo produced an excellent shot onto the 18th green. Azinger's third shot to

the 17th landed around 100 yards from the green. His fourth shot produced much better results and his ball sat safely on the 17th green. Faldo meanwhile missed a birdie on the 18th green and overshot the hole by quite a long way. By now Azinger was five under par at the 17th. Faldo shot the 18th in four leaving Azinger needing a four to tie at the 18th or a three to win the championship. Azinger failed on both counts and Faldo became the new Open Champion – his first ever.

Born on 18 July 1957 in Welwyn Garden City, Faldo originally worked as a carpet fitter and played amateur golf – he borrowed a set of clubs from his next-door neighbours to begin with – winning the British Amateur Championship and the British Youth Championship both in 1975. The following year he turned professional and gained success relatively quickly by finishing in eighth position on the European Tour order of merit in 1977 and in third place a year later. In each season he won a European Tour event and also in 1977 he was the youngest player to participate in the Ryder Cup at the age of 21. He became a leading player in the 1980s after he remodelled his swing to give him a better chance at the major tournaments. By 1987 Faldo was a strong contender and the change in swing gave him his first shot at a major championship – the Open at Muirfield – in which he claimed victory.

After his first championship during the late 1980s and throughout the entire decade to follow Faldo was the number one golfing hero in the world. He remained calm and composed under pressure and had a canny knack of intimidating his opponents which made him hard to beat. He went on to win the Masters Tournament at Augusta National Golf Club in 1989 and then again in 1990. He again won the Open Championship in that same year and then again for the third time in 1992. Faldo twice made the number one slot on the order of merit list for the European Tour in 1983 and 1992 while his earnings of more than £1.5 million that year broke all existing records.

He continued as a European Tour player and spent time in the US before deciding to concentrate his career with the PGA Tour in a bid to win further major championships. As three of these, the Masters, the US Amateur and the US Open are all held in the States it became impossible for Faldo to dedicate himself to the European Tour. The gamble paid off and Faldo claimed his sixth – and final championship – at the Masters in 1996.

ERNIE ELS WINS HIS FIRST US OPEN TITLE 1994

In 1994 Ernie Els established himself firmly on the golfing map with wins at the Dubai Desert Classic – where he beat the Emirates Course record in the first round with an exciting 11 under par with a score of 61 – and the Johnnie Walker World Championship along with the Sarazen World Open and the World Matchplay Championship at Wentworth. It was also the year that the South African won his first major tournament with his first US Open victory at Oakmont. The exciting three-way finish with Colin Montgomerie and Loren Roberts was nailbiting as the three professionals battled it out in what was at first an 18-hole play-off followed by a two-way, two-hole sudden death with Roberts.

Els was born in South Africa on 17 October 1969 and was nicknamed "The Big Easy" for his physical stature (he is six foot three inches) and his seemingly effortless golf swing. He was always a keen sportsman and grew up playing rugby, cricket, tennis, and golf – which he took up at the age of eight. His abilities on the tennis court were skilled and he achieved a win at the Eastern Transvaal Junior Championship when he was 13 years of age. The following year Els had earned himself a zero handicap and decided to focus all his attention on his golfing style and ability. He won the Junior World Golf Championship in San Diego, California aged 14 in 1984 where his runner-up was Phil Mickelson and the boys' category in the age 9-10 category was won by Tiger Woods! He was also awarded the Junior Springbok colours in 1984 and the State President Sports Award three years later before receiving his full Springbok colours in 1988. He turned professional one year later in 1989 winning his first professional tournament two years later on the South African Tour (now known as the Sunshine Tour).

He was ranked world number one during the late 1990s and is a truly global golfer and one of the most successful players in the history of the

ERNIE ELS WINS HIS FIRST US OPEN TITLE

game. His trophies are numerous and only his contemporary, Tiger Woods, holds more than Ernie Els. He is highly rated among the golfing fraternity and his peers and has remained in the top 10 of the sport's official world rankings for 655 consecutive weeks which is more than any other golfer has achieved since the current rankings were introduced in the mid-1980s. With his relaxed easy-going nature – which masks his truly competitive streak – Els is one of the most popular figures on the golf courses of today.

His career really took off in 1992 when aged just 22 he won three major tournaments on the South African Tour including the South African Open, the South African PGA and the South African Masters as well as three other tournaments that season. He travelled to Japan the following year to take part in – and win – the Dunlop Phoenix Tournament before his big breakthrough with the US Open materialised in 1994. The following year saw the young South African win the SA PGA for the second time along with the Bryon Nelson Classic in Dallas, US, winning the Bell's Cup while he also defended his World Matchplay Championship at Wentworth. With his win at Wentworth, Els became only the fourth player in the tournament's illustrious 32-year history to do so.

However the following year in 1996 seems to have catapulted the young star to even greater heights with his win at the South African Open Championship and an extensive schedule in the US which included the Buick Classic – which he won – along with various matches in Europe, the Far East and back home in South Africa. His historic third successive win at the World Matchplay Championship and his five-day tour in the Johnnie Walker Super Tour throughout Asia including the Philippines, Taiwan, Korea and Thailand also helped to stand the golfing hero in good stead. 1996 was also the year in which Els won the singles in the World Cup of Golf for South Africa as well as in the foursomes with fellow South African Wayne Westner.

He began his illustrious career in Australia in 1997 where he won the Johnnie Walker Classic before following it up with his second major championship – the US Open at Congressional – where he hit a stunning shot onto the formidable 17th green in the final round. It helped Els to seal his fate and he ended the tournament with a one-shot victory over Scotland's Colin Montgomerie. He went on to win the Buick Classic for a second time and the PGA Grand Slam Tournament (the tournament featuring the four major tournament winners of the year). The other winners were Tiger Woods, Davis Love III and Justin Leonard. His career continues to flourish and rise and Els was ranked world number five at the beginning of the 2007 season.

NICK FALDO WINS THE MASTERS ERASING NORMAN'S LEAD 1996

Nick Faldo and Greg Norman's confrontation in the final round at the 1996 Masters at Augusta National was truly one of the most memorable "duels" witnessed by spectators and the golfing fraternity alike. Norman had completed three exceptional days at the tournament and began the final round six shots ahead of Faldo at 13 under par. Faldo's exceptional shot from the tee of the par three 6th hole landed within inches of the hole on the green and his putt for a birdie was delivered in style. Norman got his par but Faldo was now eight under par and only four strokes behind his rival.

Both competitors completed a par four at the 7th and Norman managed a par five at the 8th while Faldo completed a birdie and halved the leading score. Worse was to come for Norman when his shot at the 9th rolled off the green and back onto the sloping fairway. Faldo retaliated with another birdie and was then just two shots behind the leader. Norman then missed the green at the 10th while Faldo made a solid par. Things were beginning to change. The excitement was building as the lead was down to one stroke. The final holes were going to prove a challenge for both men.

At the 12th hole Faldo took the lead when Norman's shot over the lake failed to make the green and rolled slowly but surely off the green into the waters of the lake that promptly swallowed the "Shark's" ball. Faldo at this point was nine under par while the Australian trailed behind for the first time in the tournament at seven under. Faldo continued on form and made a good shot to the green at the 16th. Norman's shot however found the dangerously placed lake beside the green. The "Shark" was forced to take a penalty third shot to the green – it was a beautiful shot but by now the Australian was realising that his Masters victory was quickly slipping out of his grasp. Faldo's putt swung wide of the hole and his ball settled roughly 20 inches away from the cup. Norman suffered the same fate and although both players reached par at the

17th the contest was basically over. At the 18th Faldo was convincingly four shots in the lead despite having to chip the shot out of a difficult bunker. It was to be his day though when the previously wayward ball landed beautifully on the green with literally a yard or so between the hole and the player's third Masters victory. An excellent putt from Faldo meant it was all over for Norman.

The two men embraced on the 18th green and Faldo received his Green Jacket for the third time. He had won the tournament by five strokes with a five under par 67. It made him the sixth player to win three Masters Tournaments and he joined the likes of Sam Snead, Jimmy Demaret, Gary Player, Jack Nicklaus and Arnold Palmer.

Faldo had won the Masters despite a number of issues that could have made the outcome particularly difficult. He was suffering from painful shoulder spasms. Professionally he was smarting from having missed the cut at the Players Championship two weeks prior to the Masters in 1996 and he was further compounded by the break-up of his 10-year marriage and subsequent divorce. Perhaps that he was not quite on form was evidenced when he failed to make a mark at any of the major championships the previous year. He had finished outside the top 20 in all four major events.

Suffering from a bout of self-doubt, Faldo did not expect to win the Masters in 1996 and many people agreed with him feeling that the favourite Norman was bound to claim the title. So how did the British player with the world on his shoulders come back from a six-stroke deficit to claim the first major tournament of the season?

The first round saw him paired with John Daly who drove Faldo on at every hole. Despite Daly's form, Faldo shot the lower score and ended the round on 67 to Daly's 71 – at this his 13th Masters, it was his first under-70 score in three years and it gave Faldo a boost. Norman was leading the field with a first-round score of 63. The following day saw Faldo paired with Brad Faxon and again he achieved a 67 leaving him four shots behind Norman who was in the lead on 69. The final day saw Faldo six shots down and paired with Norman. He secretly believed he could have a chance at the championship and challenge his rival to victory. The two had never really become firm friends due to the pressure of rivalry that existed between them following their meeting at the 1990 Open where their pairing in the final round saw Faldo defeat the "Shark" in a 67-76 win. The run of bad luck and mistakes made by Norman on the final day of the Masters in 1996 gave Faldo his chance and his five under par victory will be forever etched in the memories of the golfing world and not least the man with the troubles himself.

TIGER WOODS WINS THE MASTERS BY 12 STROKES, AS A PRO 1997

It must have seemed like a miracle when rookie Tiger Woods pulled off a 12-stroke lead to win the Masters Tournament in 1997 in his first professional event. No one was surprised when he reclaimed Augusta for the US in record-breaking fashion at the tournament a year after turning professional. His sponsors were so confident in his success that they had already paid him $60 million when he turned professional in August 1996. He won the tournament 18 under par. His closest rival was Tom Kite at six under par. His stunning performance was remarkable.

Tiger Woods has golf in his blood. He began playing at the age of two and quickly became a child prodigy. At the age of three he putted with Bob Hope in a television appearance on The Mike Douglas Show and at the same age shot a score of 48 over nine holes at the Navy Golf Club in Cypress, California. Born on 30 December 1975 in Cypress, Eldrick Woods was nicknamed "Tiger" after a friend of his father who served with him in Vietnam. He is the youngest of his father's four children and the only child from his father's marriage to his mother Kultida. He first appeared in Golf Digest aged five and went on to win the boys' category in the 9-10 age group at the Junior World Championships – he was only eight years old. He won the championship six times in all including four consecutive wins between 1988 and 1991.

By the age of 15 he became the youngest US Junior Amateur Champion in golf's history which he successfully defended in 1992. Also in 1992 Woods entered and competed in his first PGA Tour event at the Los Angeles Open. Then in 1993 he won his third consecutive US Junior Amateur Championship.

The following year was to see Woods become the youngest US Amateur Champion. His outstanding career grew from strength to strength and the awards and accolades are too numerous to mention. The year 1995 saw Woods as the only amateur to make the cut and to appear in the Masters where he tied in 41st place. Then in 1996 aged just 20 he went on

TIGER WOODS WINS THE MASTERS BY 12 STROKES, AS A PRO

GREATEST MOMENTS OF GOLF

to become the first golfer in the history of the sport to win three consecutive US Amateur titles. His first professional tournament was the Greater Milwaukee Open and despite tying in 60th place he won other tournaments and qualified for the Tour Championship. In his first year as a professional he was named as 1996's "Sportsman of the Year" by Sports Illustrated and Rookie of the Year by the PGA Tour.

His influence on golf has been monumental and his impact, particularly in the US, unique. His record win at the Masters in 1997 made him the youngest ever winner of the major tournament and the first winner of African/Asian descent. He set 20 Masters records and tied six further records which has led him to become the most prolific golfer in the world – perhaps the most prolific golfer in the history of the game.

In less than a year of being a professional the young player from California was named the number one golfer in the Official World Golf Rankings – he holds the record for getting to the top slot in just 42 weeks. But Woods' fortunes turned the following year when he only won one PGA Tour event. Woods himself put it down to the changes he was making in his swing. Like great golfers before him changes in style take time and effort and often result in a lack of previous form before a new breed of player is unleashed.

By June 1999 Woods was back – as predicted – on top form and his win at the Memorial tournament perhaps marked the beginning of what was to become a prolonged period of dominance in the world of golf. He achieved 17 wins at PGA tournaments over 24 months and went on to claim a further 32 victories over the next five seasons. By the end of the 1990s Woods was a phenomenon and ended the 1999 season with eight convincing wins. He became the PGA Tour Player of the Year and remained in the top 10 of the Official World Golf Rankings for 264 consecutive weeks.

Woods also proved himself a record-breaker when he beat Old Tom Morris's score of 1862 to win the biggest victory margin in a major championship when he won the 2000 US Open at Pebble Beach with a 15-stroke lead. That year also saw Woods in exceptional form, he began the season with a fifth consecutive victory and he won the Open on the Old Course at St Andrews with a convincing eight-stroke win. The mighty player also set a new record when he completed the course in the lowest ever score in a major championship finishing 19 under par. With his Open victory came another accolade – Woods became the youngest ever player to achieve a Grand Slam.

PAYNE STEWART WINS US OPEN AND LATER TRAGICALLY DIES 1999

It was a tragedy that shocked the golfing community and the world at large when Payne Stewart, who had just won the US Open, was killed in a plane crash on 25 October 1999. Both pilots and all four passengers perished when the Lear jet they were travelling in came down over the north west of the US. Bound from Orlando to Dallas the plane had strayed off course over north Florida before continuing in a northeasterly direction and seemingly running out of fuel. Investigators confirmed that the cockpit windows were frosted over which seemed consistent with a loss of pressure and a subsequent rapid drop in temperature. Many experts believe that the pilots and passengers would have lost consciousness due to a lack of oxygen or to hypoxia although when the aircraft last made communication with air traffic control it was reportedly flying at around 45,000 feet. Stewart won the US Open that year at Pebble Beach when he made a 15-foot putt on the last hole beating Phil Mickelson by one stroke. It was the first time that a professional player had made that kind of shot on the last hole to win a major tournament.

It was a disaster that rocked the golfing fraternity and abruptly ended the life of a major sporting hero at the young age of 42. Born on 30 January 1957 in Springfield, Missouri, Stewart was an entertaining player renowned for his golfing wardrobe alongside his golf. He favoured a colourful uniform of tam o'shanter caps, patterned trousers – including plus fours – and knickerbockers which made him an instant target for the golfing media. A month before his untimely death Stewart had competed in the 1999 Ryder Cup and the plane he boarded that fateful day was taking him to the Tour Championship – the last tournament of the season. Popular with fans, Stewart put in a remarkable performance at the 1999 US Open which was sadly to be his last major

PAYNE STEWART WINS US OPEN AND LATER TRAGICALLY DIES

tournament. It was the third of three majors that the American would achieve in his short but exciting lifetime.

It all began for Stewart back in the late 1970s when he failed to make the PGA Tour. This resulted in him playing on the Asian tour for a couple of years – where he was champion on two occasions before gaining his PGA Tour card in 1982. That same year saw the up and coming player achieve his first win at the Quad Cities Open. He went on to win 11 tour events – including the PGA Championship in 1989 – along with the US Open in 1991 and 1999. He participated in the Ryder Cup on five occasions in 1987, 1989, 1991, 1993 and 1999 and was a dedicated and patriotic team member. Renowned for his team spirit he was also picked to play for three US World Cup teams.

His death was hard for his contemporaries to take and the 1999 Tour Championship – which he'd been travelling to when he was killed – was opened by a lone bagpipes playing "Amazing Grace". Most PGA events are filled with glamour, prestige and money, but the 1999 event was marred by Stewart's death. Life goes on and so does the PGA but the final tournament of the season was a sombre affair and Tiger Woods won with little or no fanfare. Many of the players paid tribute to Stewart by wearing plus fours and caps although the first day of the tour was put aside for a memorial service to take place in Orlando. Throughout the tournament Stewart was never far from anyone's mind. When Tiger Woods finished with his 15th top 10 win of the year it was an eerie reminder that Stewart himself was the last man to top that number when he achieved 16 top finishes in 1986. Polite applause replaced the usual roar of the crowds.

The following year at the 2000 US Open – where Stewart would have been defending his title had he lived – saw 21 of his former friends and team-mates and professionals hit golf balls into the Pacific Ocean from the Pebble Beach Course in a golfing version of the 21 Gun Salute. In 2001 Stewart was posthumously inducted into the World Golf Hall of Fame. The 2005 US Open once again returned to Pinehurst – where Stewart won the championship in 1999 – and the event was filled with tributes and remembrance of the great man while a bronze statue of Stewart was unveiled near the 18th green. Stewart was survived by his wife Tracey and their two children. The PGA Tour set up a First Tee programme in Stewart's home state Missouri to help disadvantaged youngsters learn to play golf.

TIGER WOODS, HOLDS ALL FOUR MAJOR TITLES AT ONCE 2001

It was an exciting year for Tiger Woods and one that would set the pace for things to come. He had already won three major tournaments the previous year and was the only player since Ben Hogan in 1953 to achieve that particular accolade. Soon after his narrow victory over Bob May in the 2000 PGA Championship at Valhalla in Louisville, Woods also joined in Lee Trevino's record in 1971 as the only other player to achieve three National Opens in one year including the US Open, the Open and the Canadian Open. But it was his 2001 Masters win that was to give Woods a Grand Slam and make him the only winner of this prestigious title to be the holder of all four major championships at the same time within the modern era of the Grand Slam. The first man to achieve such a feat – as an amateur – was Bobby Jones in 1930 although Woods did not quite achieve all four majors in one season as Jones did. Woods' win at St Andrews on the Old Course was his second major victory in a run of consecutive wins following his win at the US Open earlier in 2000. Woods was 19 under par for a birdie putt on the 18th.

Tiger Woods' achievement of holding all four major titles at the same time became known as the "Tiger Slam" and although he didn't excel at the three other majors that season – the PGA Championship, the US Open and the Open – he did finish the tour with the most PGA tour wins of the season with a total of five victories. 2002 also started strongly for Woods and he once again triumphed at the Masters in Augusta and became only the third man to achieve successive wins at Bobby Jones' course following in the footsteps of Jack Nicklaus who won in 1965 and 1966 and Nick Faldo who repeated the feat in 1989 and 1990. At the 2002 US Open he was the only player under par. The expectation on Woods to pull off a Grand Slam in one season was high, but the champion of champions found the title eluded him when he finished his final round at the Open with a score of 81. The PGA Championship was lost to Woods by one stroke after bogeys at the 13th and 14th holes. If he had won he would once again have achieved three majors in one season – although despite disappointment he did take home the Player of the Year award for the fourth consecutive year running. He was also at the top of the money list and won the Vardon Trophy.

TIGER WOODS, HOLDS ALL FOUR MAJOR TITLES AT ONCE

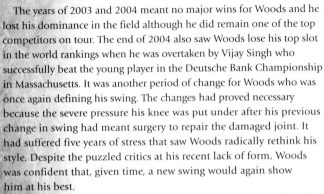

The years of 2003 and 2004 meant no major wins for Woods and he lost his dominance in the field although he did remain one of the top competitors on tour. The end of 2004 also saw Woods lose his top slot in the world rankings when he was overtaken by Vijay Singh who successfully beat the young player in the Deutsche Bank Championship in Massachusetts. It was another period of change for Woods who was once again defining his swing. The changes had proved necessary because the severe pressure his knee was put under after his previous change in swing had meant surgery to repair the damaged joint. It had suffered five years of stress that saw Woods radically rethink his style. Despite the puzzled critics at his recent lack of form, Woods was confident that, given time, a new swing would again show him at his best.

He was proved right at the start of the 2005 season when he beat Phil Mickelson at the Doral Championship and reclaimed his number one slot in the world rankings. He went on to win the first major tournament of the season – the Masters. Over the following months Woods and Singh swapped the number one slot in the world rankings a number of times but Woods propelled himself forward when he won the Open Championship (his 10th major tournament win). By this time Woods was engaged – and had been for a couple of years – to Swedish model Elin Nordegren. The couple had been introduced by Swedish golf star Jesper Parnevik who had employed Nordegren as a nanny for the Open Championship in 2001. Tiger Woods and Elin Nordegren were married on 5 October 2004 and set up home in Windermere, a suburb in Orlando, Florida.

Tiger Woods' popularity is such that he has done just as much as Arnold Palmer before him to bring golf to a wider audience. Perhaps due to his ethnic background more and more young players are emerging in the US who feel an affinity with the young star who at the age of 30 has broken more records, set more records and held more accolades than any other golfer in the history of the game.

EUROPE WINS THE RYDER CUP AFTER AN EPIC FINAL DAY 2002

The 34th Ryder Cup was scheduled for the Belfry once again and the two teams – from the US and Europe – were as ever both anxious for victory. The 24 players that made up the teams gave their all and each match was a fierce competition that ended in victory for the European team. Sam Torrance's team had claimed a 15½-12½ triumph that culminated in a huge party for both teams at the end of the third day.

The Irishman Paul McGinley was instrumental in the final outcome when he putted 11 feet for the hole on the 18th green. Like many before him he was the hero of the hour including Christy O'Connor Jr in 1989 at the Belfry, Philip Walton in 1995 at Oak Hill and Costantino Rocca in 1997 at Valderrama. The Belfry had also been the setting when in 1985 Sam Torrance himself had been the one to putt the ball at the 18th for a deciding win over the US. The final day was full of tension and the singles matches were dramatic. The three-point lead was also the European team's biggest marginal win over the US since Sam Torrance's performance nearly 20 years earlier.

At the start of the final day the scores were level at eight each. Torrance decided to send in the "big guns" first in order to gain points and step up momentum. The formula proved to be a good strategy as Colin Montgomerie won by one stroke over his American counterpart Scott Hoch. Bernhard Langer won his match against Hal Sutton while Padraig Harrington added a further point when he defeated Mark Calcavecchia. Darren Clarke also won his match against David Duval although Sergio Garcia conceded to David Toms by one stroke. Scott Verplank then triumphed over Lee Westwood and the European team were only two points ahead.

The excitement mounted as Niclas Fasth, who matched Paul Azinger's game across all 18 greens, stepped onto the course for Europe. However the experienced American managed to gain an extra half point at the end of the match. Phillip Price was

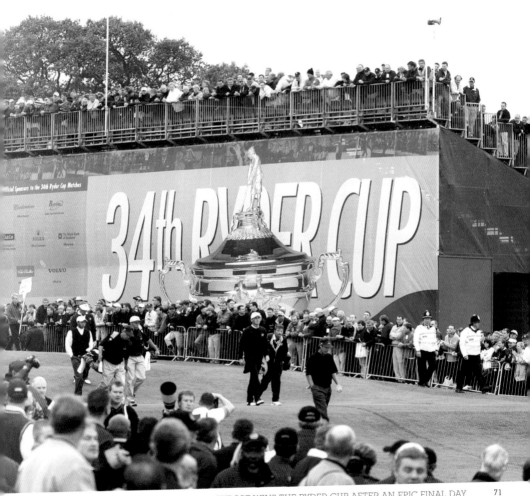

EUROPE WINS THE RYDER CUP AFTER AN EPIC FINAL DAY

decidedly a hero when he won over Phil Mickelson. Swede Pierre Fulke gained a half point against Davis Love III and Jesper Parnevik – also from Sweden – managed another half when Tiger Woods conceded a four-foot par putt on the 18th green. All was left to play for and the pressure fell on rookie McGinley to perform. For most of his match against Jim Furyk, McGinley was trailing behind the American giant – he needed just a half point to win for Europe. He putted a birdie four at the 17th to level the scores and with his sensational 11-foot putt he ensured that the Ryder Cup would be travelling east across the North Atlantic Ocean.

It seems that as captain Torrance was inspirational. He had conversed with Manchester United manager Sir Alex Ferguson and the former golfing star readily acknowledges that he learnt a great deal from Fergie. One of the most important tips that Sir Alex passed on was that there are no major players, no superstars in a team. Everyone is just as crucial as the next person and that's the way Torrance decided to play it. Part of Torrance's preparations included speaking to players individually a number of times and often at great lengths. He spoke to all the players on the putting green before the match began and he also walked all 12 players to the first tee.

Colin Montgomerie was also a leading factor in the European side's inspirational edge. He remained calm and relaxed and provided a backbone that held the team together and focused. Sam Torrance was particularly impressed with Monty's approach. Bernhard Langer was also another foundation for the team to build on and showed his abilities as a leader when he suggested that Paul McGinley take the first shot when Darren Clarke found himself in a bunker. The excellent shot from McGinley put the pressure on the US partnership of Scott Hoch and Jim Furyk. Colin Montgomerie also obtained four and a half points out of five and earned himself much praise for the steadfast lead he gave the rest of the team.

Despite defeat, US captain Curtis Strange remained upbeat remarking that although it was disappointing to lose the match it certainly didn't spoil the event and he readily agreed that the European team had played better golf than the US side.

The outstanding players of the match were undoubtedly Montgomerie who was only the third man (following the two Spaniards, Ballesteros and Olazabal) to gain a score of four and a half while David Toms was the best American rookie (along with Chip Beck) with a final score of three and a half points. Both Thomas Bjorn and Padraig Harrington remained undefeated in Ryder Cup singles while Jim Furyk remained unbeaten in his three singles games with two and a half points out of three. Phillip Price gave Phil Mickelson his first singles defeat and Bernhard Langer repeated his 1985 success in the singles over Hal Sutton.

ANNIKA SORENSTAM CONTESTS A PGA TOUR EVENT 2003

As for many years, since her professional career began back in 1993, Annika Sorenstam (born on 9 October 1970 in Sweden) ended 2002 as the indisputable top women's golfer of the year. Her earnings were reported to be nearly £3 million and she set a new record scoring average of 68.7 securing herself an induction into the LPGA Hall of Fame. But 2003 was to prove a testing year for Sorenstam when she made her debut on the PGA tour.

The year began with five LPGA events during the opening months where she registered five top 10 finishes including her win at the Office Depot Championship. However Sorenstam then announced that she was to play in the Fort Worth at Hogan's Alley having been invited to participate by the organisers of the Colonial. There were mixed feelings about Sorenstam's involvement, from Vijay Singh's outspoken concern that a woman was being allowed to take part in a man's competition, to those who supported the world's leading lady. Despite trying to ignore and avoid the rising controversy, Sorenstam herself admitted that rather than wanting to make a stand for women's golf she was merely wanting to test the limits of her own game. Had Sorenstam been a man her achievements would probably have hit the headlines and praise for the leading golfer would have been high. Spurred on by the mediocre attention she received Sorenstam was probably keen to prove her worth at the next level in sporting achievement.

Sorenstam was widely supported by the crowd that attended on day one when she walked towards the first tee, even if some fellow competitors were not. Her playing partners were also in full support as both Aaron Barber and Dean Wilson declared themselves honoured to be a part of history in the making. Both men helped to calm the nervous woman player and Sorenstam soon settled into a comfortable game. Her first round was fairly typical of her excellent previous performances but the pressure of playing in front of huge crowds was clearly visible by the second round. It was as though the world's number one was trying to please the crowds and hampered by nerves never really found herself in her stride. Indeed Sorenstam almost had to catch up to make par. She ended up with a succession of bogeys leading to a score of 74. Despite being the end of

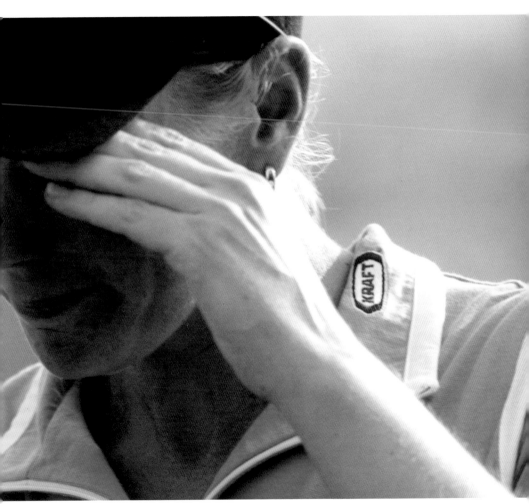

ANNIKA SORENSTAM CONTESTS A PGA TOUR EVENT

GREATEST MOMENTS OF GOLF

Sorenstam's stab at the tournament she received the largest standing ovation of the event. The world's leading woman golfer was overwhelmed – unusually – by emotion and stated later that although the experience had been exhilarating she would not be contesting the Colonial in the future. The shame was that too many critics – including fellow competitors – uttered a collective huge sigh of relief.

Annika Sorenstam began playing golf at the age of 12 supported by her parents and her sister Lotta Sorenstam (also a professional golfer). In 1995 she won the Athlete of the Year Award – Sweden's most prestigious sports award. She enjoyed a successful amateur career and was a member of the Swedish national team between 1987 and 1992. Sorenstam became the World Amateur Champion in 1992 and came in at second place in the US Women's Amateur Championship.

In her first year as a professional in 1993, Sorenstam found herself Rookie of the Year on the European Tour. Her major tournaments include the 1995 US Women's Open, the 1996 US Women's Open, the 1997 Chrysler-Plymouth Tournament of Champions, the Michelob Light Classic in 1998 and then again in 1999. Sorenstam also won the 2000 Welch's/Circle K Championship which she won again the following year along with the Nabisco Championship and the 2002 LPGA Takefuji Classic. This prolific player has also competed in the Solheim Cup representing Europe in 1994, 1996, 1998, 2000, 2002, 2003 and 2005. On 9 August 2002 Sorenstam missed the cut at the Women's British Open at Turnberry which was her first missed cut in 74 tournaments since she missed the US Open in 1999.

Sorenstam is clearly one of the most successful women golfers in the world. She has won 69 official LPGA tournaments which include an impressive 10 major tournaments. Between 2000 and 2005 she won at least five tournaments each year and this leading player tops the LPGA's career money list by several million dollars and is estimated to have earnings of more than $20 million. Sorenstam is also the holder of a number of scoring records including the lowest score in a single round which she achieved at the 2001 Standard Register PING tournament with a staggering score of 59. She has also won the Vare Trophy six times which is given to the player with the lowest scoring average in a season.

During her educational years Sorenstam moved to the US where she played collegiate golf for the University of Arizona. Sorenstam had an exceptional year and added more impressive wins to her already impressive record. She defended her title in the MasterCard Classic in 2006 and won the US Women's Open along with the Women's World Cup of Golf for Sweden with partner Liselotte Neumann.

TODD HAMILTON WINS THE OPEN IN A PLAY-OFF WITH ELS 2004

It was a gripping finale to the 2004 Open Championship that Todd Hamilton won after a four-hole play-off with South African Ernie Els. Hamilton was up by one stroke at the 133rd Open hosted at Royal Troon in Scotland. It was a first time major win for Hamilton who had been posted by the bookies as a 250-1 outsider who had to face the challenge of Els and Phil Mickelson. Mickelson was nine under after the par putt at the 18th for a score of 68. With a final score of 73-66-68-68 Mickelson had put in an outstanding performance. Hamilton was 11 under par at the 16th and two strokes ahead of Els who completed the hole nine under par. Hamilton missed the birdie putt at the 17th while his score remained at 11 under par.

Els put in a fine performance at the 17th making a birdie putt to put his score one behind Hamilton at 10 under par. His tee shot from the 18th was absolutely perfect and Hamilton faced increased pressure as the tension in the spectator stands began to mount. Hamilton's ball from the tee at the 18th landed in the rough in ground that was notorious for some who had had the misfortune to play from the spot before, although other players had been lucky when they chipped the ball out and it wasn't impossible to reach the green. Unfortunately for Hamilton, his confident looking chip from the rough took his ball to the other side of the fairway and into the spectators watching along the rough.

Els meanwhile at 10 under par only had another 175 yards to his final hole. His beautiful shot took the ball comfortably onto the green although he was rather unlucky when the ball rolled over a slight ridge to put him around 12 yards short. Hamilton had better luck with his next shot which took the ball onto the green. His par putt at 11 under at the 18th went slightly left of the hole and it left Ernie Els with the chance to putt for the Open Championship. However he missed when the putt wasn't hard enough to sink the ball and it rolled on the sloping edge to the right of

TODD HAMILTON WINS THE OPEN IN A PLAY-OFF WITH ELS

the hole. Els scored a final round of 68. Hamilton's tap-in meant a play-off loomed for the two legendary players.

Hamilton looked calm and confident as he went into the play-off with Els. Els was aiming for a par putt at the 17th hole but was disappointed to fall just short. Hamilton was in the lead by one stroke as the players headed off to the 18th hole. Ernie Els made the green in two strokes while Todd Hamilton made it in three. His final shot from the fairway was remarkable and gave him a good shot on the green. Despite a concerted effort Els missed the birdie putt at the 18th while Hamilton calmly put the ball in the hole to claim the Open Championship.

Hamilton's victory was the second consecutive year that an unheralded player from the US had won the Open Championship. Todd Hamilton's win meant that he is exempt in the Open until he reaches 66. He is also exempt from the PGA Tour for five years (between 2005 and 2010) and he is also exempt on the Masters and the US Open for five years from the time of his win.

Hamilton grew up in Oquawka on the Mississippi. He was born in Galesburg in west central Illinois on 18 October 1965. He played golf regularly on the local nine-hole course at Hend-Co Hills (now an 18-hole course) and he turned professional in 1987 but was not eligible for the PGA Tour card. This resulted in Hamilton playing internationally for many years – mostly in Japan on the golf tour there. When he left the Japan Golf Tour he was the all-time leading non-Japanese money winner with earnings in excess of more than 630 million yen having won the championship 11 times. Hamilton tried a further eight times to gain access onto the PGA Tour but to no avail. Eventually he went back to qualifying school in 2003 and he finally managed to obtain the card that had remained so elusive to him. The Honda Classic was his first PGA Tour win when he birdied the 17th and 18th holes to beat Davis Love III by one stroke at 12 under par.

Before Hamilton was eligible to join the PGA Tour he had some exciting wins including the 1994 Thailand Open, the 1992 Singapore Rolex Masters and the Maekyung Open. He also achieved wins at various tournaments between 1992 and 2003 on the Japan Golf Tour including the 1993 Acom International, the 1995 Token Corporation Cup, the 1996 PGA Philanthropy Tournament and the 1998 Gene Sarazen Classic.

GEOFF OGILVY CLAIMS THE US OPEN BY ONE SHOT
2006

Geoff Ogilvy was born on 11 June 1977 in Adelaide, South Australia. He became a professional golfer in May 1998 and won a European tour card in the same year after finishing qualifying school. The year 1999 saw him playing on the European Tour where he finished in 65th position in his first season. The following year he finished in 48th place and went on to join the US PGA tour in 2001. Ogilvy finished in the top 100 in each of his first five seasons and his first win at a professional tournament came in 2005 at the Chrysler Classic in Tuscon. The start of the 2006 season was promising for Ogilvy when he won the WGC Accenture Match Play Championship in February beating golfing great Davis Love III. He became the first Australian to win a major tournament since Steve Elkington won the PGA Championship in 1995 when he won the US Open in 2006.

Ogilvy finished with improbable pars on the 17th and 18th holes – he chipped a 30-foot shot at the 17th and then worked for par at the 18th with a downhill six-foot shot for his final stroke. Like Campbell the previous year, Ogilvy surprised the golfing fraternity and his competitors when he came from outside to win the championship.

The final play between Ogilvy, Phil Mickelson and Colin Montgomerie was mesmerising and both championship players needed pars at the 18th or bogeys to tie with the Australian. But chances for the two sporting heroes were ruined when they both produced double bogeys while Jim Furyk who just needed a par to force a play-off ended up with a bogey at the final hole. Ogilvy claimed a dramatic win which propelled him into the Official World Golf Rankings top 10 for the first time in his professional career coming in at number eight. He was ranked number seven by July 2006.

GEOFF OGILVY CLAIMS THE US OPEN BY ONE SHOT

At the 106th US Open in 2006, Ogilvy just wasn't expected to win. The man himself didn't expect to win either. But a series of improbable events over the back nine holes led the young player to his championship title at Winged Foot. It was the first time that an Australian had won the US Open since David Graham had won the championship at Merion Golf Club in Ardmore in 1981.

The tournament was a brutal four days for the young professional who at 29 years of age had never come close to such a dream before. Five US Opens have been hosted at the prestigious Winged Foot course and Ogilvy managed to obtain the third lowest score after Hale Irwin in 1974 and Bobby Jones in 1929 with his five over par 285. Ranked in 21st place for the week of the tournament Ogilvy didn't believe he had a chance of a win.

It was his ability to maintain par over the final four holes – which none of the other competitors achieved that gave him his historic win. As much as Ogilvy will be remembered for winning the tournament, Phil Mickelson will also be remembered for the tournament he gave away when his two-stroke lead slipped away from him over the last three holes. Mickelson's bogey at the 16th and his double bogey on the final hole meant that the mighty man of golf kissed goodbye to any chance of a triumphant victory and any chance he had that season of gaining a magnificent Grand Slam. Mickelson had taken the lead at the 14th when he made birdie giving him a two-stroke lead over Montgomerie, Ogilvy, Harrington and Furyk. Another possible winner had been Furyk. He was partnered with Harrington and was not far off securing his second US Open championship in four years but a bogey at the par 4 15th didn't help and neither did the par putt that slid away from the champion at the final hole.

Before the unpredictable result at the US Open in 2006 where Phil Mickelson walked off the 18th green in disbelief at the double bogey he had just played, Ogilvy's previous accolades include the 1998-99 Australasian PGA Tour Rookie of the Year, Best Amateur Performances winner 1998 and the Tasmanian Open winner 1998. He was also the Mandurah Easter Open winner 1998 and the Queensland Medal winner 1997 as well as the Victorian Amateur Champion winner 1997 and the Lake Macquarie winner 1997. He also previously won a Queensland Medal in 1996 and stormed the German Amateur Championship that same year.

TIGER WOODS WINS THE OPEN AFTER FATHER'S DEATH 2006

The setting was the Open Tournament hosted by Royal Liverpool. It had been 39 years since the Open had been held at the course and it proved to be an emotional occasion for Tiger Woods who championed to victory not long after the death of his greatest inspiration – his father Earl Woods who died aged 74 in May 2006. The reason that Earl Woods and his wife, Tiger Woods' mother had encouraged their son to play golf was so that he would be confident and have a good life. They had not set out to turn the young child prodigy into a major champion but their foresight, love and their encouragement had done just that. Earl Woods was undoubtedly the driving force and major inspiration behind his son's phenomenal career. His son later stated: "My dad was my best friend and greatest role model and I will miss him deeply."

Woods Senior was diagnosed with prostate cancer in 1998 which was treated with radiation following a heart bypass a decade earlier. The cancer returned and spread throughout the mentor's body and at the beginning of 2006 he was too frail to travel to the Masters Tournament for the first time. Father and son had an extremely close bond and Earl Woods' enthusiasm for his son's talent and the encouragement and support that he gave was quite simply second to none.

Earl Woods was not a zealous father; he was a mentor, architect and driving force who delighted in what his son achieved. He was instrumental in Tiger Woods becoming the professional he is today and was pro-active in his approach to his son's career. He had carried out two tours in Vietnam and was the first black man to play baseball in the Big Eight Conference. His death at his home in Cypress, California came as a devastating blow to his 30-year-old son.

With his grief still raw but his professionalism intact, Tiger Woods stepped onto the course at Royal Liverpool to compete in the Open. The 135th Open Championship was taking place on links that had previously been described as out of date but as play over four days proved – Hoylake is a long way off being taken off the Championship calendar. Strategy was the order of the day on the difficult links course which challenges even the most experienced of professionals. All were jockeying for position on day one but on day two there was a clear contention for the title between

TIGER WOODS WINS THE OPEN AFTER FATHER'S DEATH 87

TIGER WOODS WINS THE OPEN AFTER FATHER'S DEATH

Tiger Woods and Ernie Els. But Hoylake presents little margin for error and victory was anyone's at this point. The second day proved a positive one for the likes of Els, DiMarco and Goosen but Woods was still in with a chance of success.

Day three saw Sergio Garcia and Ernie Els with Chris DiMarco one shot off the leader, Woods. Jim Furyk and Angel Cabrera also played well despite the uneven pace of the course. The final day saw Tiger Woods reign supreme despite fierce opposition, a difficult course and the personal tragedy that he took around the 72 holes with him. It was a testament to the truly professional golfer that he is and the victory was well deserved.

When victory was his Tiger Woods broke down and sobbed openly on the shoulder of his caddy Steve Williams and then found the arms of his wife Elin as he walked off the green. When Woods was presented with the famous claret jug on sealing his championship victory he was unsure of what to say at the presentation ceremony. Woods who received the claret jug for the third time in his illustrious career for his five under par 67 and a total score of 18 under par 270 began by stating that it had been a fantastic week. He mentioned that the course was in excellent condition and he thanked the staff on behalf of all the players for "…one of the greatest championships ever staged." He went on to say that his father had been with him and had kept him calm throughout the tournament. He also felt that his performance on the final day had been his best in the championship. He also made a special mention about Ryder Cup team-mate Chris DiMarco who himself lost his mother earlier the same month.

When Tiger Woods prepared to return to the PGA Tour one month later it was still clear that he had yet to come to terms with the death of his father. He stated to reporters that what had been particularly hard for him to swallow was the fact he hadn't won the Masters at Augusta in 2006 as this was the last tournament his father had seen him play. It hurt him greatly that the last major tournament his father had watched did not result in a victory. Woods was about to participate in the Buick Open which presented him with several different challenges. Also 2006 was a bitter-sweet moment for Woods who went on to become golf's dominant figure that year despite his tragic loss.

EUROPE EQUAL RECORD POINTS VICTORY IN THE RYDER CUP 2006

No one thought it was possible. No one thought that the European team would even win the Ryder Cup in 2006, much less achieve a repeat of their historic victory score of 18½ to 9½ two years earlier, yet the team, captained by Ian Woosnam did exactly that at the K Club in Ireland designed by American Arnold Palmer who built the Palmer Course and the Smurfit Course. These two beautiful courses were designed with championship golf in mind and many thought that the layout was much more suited to the US team than the European one. The European team obviously didn't think so.

The two on-course leaders who championed the Europeans to victory were Darren Clarke and Colin Montgomerie. Montgomerie had already proved his worth as a leader in the previous match and was inspirational along with Clarke and captain Woosnam. It was a winning combination and each member of the European team contributed to the points during the first two days of foursomes and fourballs matches. The singles on the final day were particularly awe-inspiring with Woosnam's team romping home with a final singles victory of eight and a half points to three and a half. However it started on the Friday with a resounding lead from the European team who didn't let their guard down for a moment and who dominated the first day's play.

Ian Woosnam stuck with his earlier winning strategy – employed in 2004 – and sent Colin Montgomerie out first in the singles matches on the final day to set a standard for the remaining team members to follow. Montgomerie's role was also to inspire his own team while intimidating their opponents from across the Atlantic and obviously the plan worked. His game with David Toms was a nerve-racking game that eventually saw the Scotsman finish with a one-hole lead over his American rival. The result was an amazing unbeaten record of eight singles match wins for the outstanding player from north of the border.

The win was truly magnificent and Europe were once again on course for an outstanding victory. Two more points were won when European team member Paul Casey defeated Jim Furyk, and David Howell – Casey's team-mate – scored a successful triumph over Brett Wetterich. Robert

EUROPE EQUAL RECORD POINTS VICTORY IN THE RYDER CUP

Karlsson lost to Tiger Woods but Sergio Garcia won his match against a highly skilled Stewart Cink who put in an impressive performance. Although it didn't all hinge on the final hole as it had done for so many past European champions including Sam Torrance and Paul McGinley, there was some pressure on the fifth-match players Luke Donald for Europe and Chad Campbell for the US to secure the next point. Donald's victory over Campbell on the 17th green ensured Europe's victory and retained the Ryder Cup for the European team. However it was far from over and Henrik Stenson – another European hero – made the winning shot with a seven-foot putt on the 15th. At the exact same time Darren Clarke was playing for the 16th and had a three-stroke cushion over opponent Zach Johnson.

It was an emotionally charged moment for the Irishman who had recently lost his wife Heather to cancer. Johnson conceded the match when he failed to convert his birdie. The home crowd gave their fellow countryman a deafening roar of approval which proved too much for the grieving Clarke. He broke down in tears and was hugged by captain Ian Woosnam and the US captain Tom Lehman as well as rival team member Tiger Woods. The emotive scene was possibly a fitting end to a triumphant Ryder Cup victory for the European team. However there were still four matches to be played.

Paul McGinley another Irishman – who had famously ensured victory in 2004 – halved with JJ Henry while Jose Maria Olazabal (the well-known half of the Olazabal/Ballesteros partnership of the 1980s and Ryder Cup veteran) defeated the world number two Phil Mickelson. Padraig Harrington was not as lucky this time round and lost to Scott Verplank. There was still the match between Westwood and DiMarco to finish. Westwood beat the American to gain another point and the European team finished with another historic 18½ point score.

The spectators on the Palmer Course were delighted with the outcome of the competition and a result that had seemed truly impossible just three days earlier. It had been an emotional three-day rollercoaster, particularly for Clarke, Woods and DiMarco who had all lost close family members in 2006. The European dominance reigns for another two years and the teams and fans alike are anxious for the next competition to take place. The 37th Ryder Cup will take place at Valhalla Golf Club in Kentucky and the European team will be captained by golfing legend Nick Faldo while the US will be captained by Paul Azinger.

ALSO AVAILABLE IN THIS SERIES

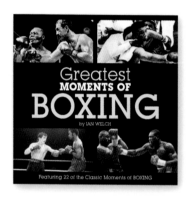

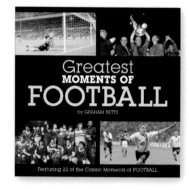

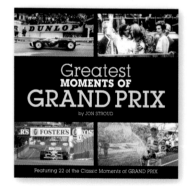

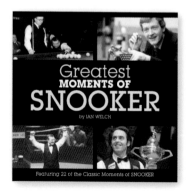

THE PICTURES IN THIS BOOK WERE PROVIDED COURTESY OF THE FOLLOWING:

GETTY IMAGES
101 Bayham Street, London NW1 0AG

Concept and Creative Direction:
VANESSA and KEVIN GARDNER

Design and Artwork: DAVID WILDISH

Image research: ELLIE CHARLESTON

PUBLISHED BY GREEN UMBRELLA PUBLISHING

Publishers:
JULES GAMMOND and VANESSA GARDNER

Written by: CLAIRE WELCH